Prairie Roots

Prairie Roots

poems by

James Lowell Hall

Shanti Arts Publishing
Brunswick, Maine

Prairie Roots

Published by Shanti Arts Publishing

Designed by Shanti Arts Designs

Cover image: Gordon Frances Muck, *Thistle*.
Used with permission.

Shanti Arts LLC
193 Hillside Road
Brunswick, Maine 04011
shantiarts.com

Printed in the United States of America

ISBN: 978-1-962082-12-9 (softcover)

Library of Congress Control Number: 2024932870

for Ruth, the keeper of tales

Lillibridge House, the home of Ray and Marguerite Lillibridge in Delavan, Illinois, built in 1915—photograph taken on its centennial in 2015

Contents

Acknowledgements

"What do you want for Christmas, Jamie?" my mother asked my four-year-old self. "People and books," I replied. And for sixty years, save one, I have gone to Delavan each Christmas season for the people. The cacophony of aunts, uncles, racing cousins— was joy for an only child. I would like to acknowledge the inspiration and debt I owe to the Lillibridge tribe, whose children and children's children journey back annually from across the country to its center in Delavan, Illinois.

None of this would be possible without Marguerite and Ray who built the first California Bungalow in Delavan and forged a lasting family. My mother, Ruth, kept the family myths and stories alive, fostering a powerful sense of belonging. She is the inspiration for this manuscript. I want to thank my wife, Jane, for her patience in listening to multiple variations of poems and for her invaluable common sense in culling the chaff. I acknowledge my children, Jamie and Lowell, who have stepped up, helping as caretakers of the Delavan home and involving the next generation, continuing the family legacy.

Thanks to Caitlin Jans who encouraged me to first publish poetry. I'm much obliged to my editors: Meghan Sterling, for her help with titles and structure, along with focusing eclectic poems into a manuscript; Judyth Hill, editor, writing coach, and mentor, for accompanying me in the painstaking journey of transforming prose into poetry, and for her love of hoboes. Thanks to members of the North Chapter poetry critique group and our leader and President of the Illinois State Poetry Society, Mary Beth Bretzlauf.

Thank you, Christine Cote, publisher of Shanti Arts, for believing in the project and creating this beautiful book.

"Prairie Fire" was first published in *Still Point Arts Quarterly,* Summer 2023.

"Lena Slack" and "When Jazz Became Swing" were first published in *The Stratford Quarterly,* Autumn 2021.

"To a Father Dying Young" was first published in The Write City Magazine, May 2023. It also appeared in the *The Write City Magazine 2023 Anthology.*

On Her Birthday . . .

My grandmother greeted
family and friends, opened letters
from three US Presidents, quoted poetry,
helped two great-grandchildren
blow out one hundred candles.

Marguerite sat in her living room, proud
of her home, proud as when Ray built it
for her, his young bride eighty years back,
first California bungalow
in their small prairie town.

She described him
with lovely laughter,
a perfect man,
gone these fifty years, still
loosening her heart to fly.

Happiness in marriage—that's not something
just happens—it's being the right partner,
not marrying the right partner.

I welcome you here, to
this, a tale of love, a tale of family—
the soul of the house that grew.

I

Prairie Dawn

burns away night mist
pollen shimmers overhead
fuses with the sun

Ray

Grew up on the plains, lived through the Children's Blizzard, prairie fires, tornadoes, the woeful sound of hateful wind, dust storms, droughts, grasshoppers that blotted out the sky, times when all the family had to eat were tomatoes and cabbage. Most of the cattle in the West died during the brutal winter of the Great Die Up. Ray survived.

Lying on thick compacted grass, nesting like a deer in cover under the flicker of lightning bugs, he dream-walked, climbed the prairie to vibrant stars overhead, his future open, unlimited.

That was before he left the Dakota Territories with nothing, save his down-home folksy sense of humor.

Childhood ended at age fourteen when Dad disappeared. Allie could not care for all her children. She sent Ray east to live with relatives in Delavan, Illinois. There he had to earn his keep, apprenticed with a carpenter, taught himself how to figure expenses and draw architectural plans, and became the town's major contractor.
Ray always was taciturn about his past. Humor helped rewind time's paradox of dreams and family.

Gee, but I am hungry. Wait a second, dear, until I pull my belt up another notch. There that's better.

So, you see, Hon, I am straighter than a string around a bundle.

You ought to see my eye, it's a peach. I am proud of it, looks like I've been kicked by a mule. You know, dear, that they can kick hard enough to knock all the soda out of a biscuit without breaking the crust.

How's every little thing been today, dear? Tell you pardner, I'm strong for my Marguerite.

Be good, and if you can't be good . . . why just be as good as you can.

Ray and Ray Jr., 1917

Rural Free Delivery (RFD)

> *Home, upon that word drops the sunshine of beauty and the shadow of tender sorrows, the reflection of ten thousand voices and fond memories.*
>
> —Ray Lillibridge

Talk about being pleased. When I
got a letter from Marguerite, I danced
a jig around the table. The room loosened
its belt, wasn't big enough to hold me.

Of all the times during the week,
being by myself is first-class.
I open a letter and have a chat with my
sweetheart, which is the next best thing
to being with her. And perhaps Marguerite

is glad to hear from a certain fellow. At least
he has many, many reasons to think so,
and to think so is to believe,
and believing is almost the truth.

What she sees to care about in him
is beyond me. But then there are a lot
of wonders and mysterious things
happening in the world.
Could your love be one of these?

This is a mighty fine old world after all
if you make yourself think so. Look happy
even if things are going against you—
that will make others happy. Pretty soon

all will be smiling and then there is no
telling what can't be done.

Marguerite Lillibridge with her students
from Meeker one-room schoolhouse, 1913

Courtship

> *That was the sweetest verse about "home." I read your letter over and over. Good night, Ray,* "mein lieges kind" *(sweet child of mine).*
>
> —Marguerite Lillibridge

Every day's a two-mile walk from Detmer's farm. I was running late in writing your Tuesday letter, so I borrowed a horse, posted letter, and made it to school just in time.

When we were getting ready to come home, an old tramp came along. It was just about dusk. I said, *good night,* and bolted. You would have thought it was Disbrow racing, if you'd seen old topsy tearing up the dust.

Ten miles as the crow flies from Hopedale to Delavan. Seems a continent apart—all the muddy, rutted roads and stuck carriages. Ray, it's good of you to bring your buggy Fridays, bringing me home to my folks. Gives time for Marguerite and Ray to have a good talk. I worry that you stay too long bringing me back Sundays. Never seems long enough when you're here, but it must be midnight when you get back to Delavan and then get up at the crack of dawn for work.

I walked two miles today through snowdrifts to the hinky-dinky schoolhouse, as you named it, lit the potbellied stove and changed my skirt and shoes, all before the children arrived. Ray, do I need a stove to warm your letters?

Yesterday hints of mint and rose wafted through the window. We went wildflower hunting in the prairie at noontime. The students gathered enough to make the top of the school library look like a flower garden, an aroma so strong it makes you hungry. Prairie roots are deep—they say as far down as an oak tree above raises its branches to the sky.

—continued

Ray and Marguerite Lillibridge, 1915

At recess the rascals convinced me to climb the cobb shed using tree branches to swing down. I gained the summit and during the breathless stillness which followed, became courageous, gave a mighty plunge, accidentally seizing the right tree limb, descending to the ground in safety, and the green grass grew around.

Sometimes it is so discouraging when you need to teach the same thing repeatedly. But there is always hope for advancement and pleasure and satisfaction later in seeing the child grow up in mind and morals, and the feeling you may have helped some, if only a trifle. Patience, Ray, sometimes I think I haven't any left, but then from some invisible power, I get a fresh supply.

There is one who always knows best, teaches us to prepare and be ready for the time when we will be taken. The Lord is good to me, Ray, the folks are well, we don't suffer from want, and dear, I have you. Surely, we ought to be exceedingly thankful.

Of all my scholars, Ray, there is one I can't help liking best—he is the dearest boy to me. Shall I tell you who he is? It's the boy that whispered something in my ear once, for the very first time, that I can never forget. Then he kissed me on my hair with a soft light caress. Do you know now? Tell him the same from me. I love you, Your Marguerite.

True Hoss

I got back Sunday night all right.
Whenever my hands got cold,
I put the charcoal foot warmer
in my lap to warm them.

Never one step out of the way
I just let the reins loose, and Dolly
made every turn in fine shape.
She's one fine hoss.

It's a new century, and the world's
changing. I need a truck
to get my men, tools, and supplies
to several work sites—rain or shine.

Mrs. Albers needs a gentle hoss
to love up, care for, and pull her buggy
from farm to town, and get her to church
Sundays, reins loose, every turn easy.

I'll miss good old Dolly,
even if she was boney.
Driving late when I nodded off,
she'd always take me home.

Made better time coming back,
she must have been thinking of her oats.

Charivari

Tonight a crowd went over
to Harvey and Edna's
to Charivari,
hunting up old cowbells to make a racket.
Marguerite stayed home.
The newlyweds came over here,
slipping out their bathroom window,
hoping to escape the worst of it,
but the gang found
them in our basement,
and made Mr. take Mrs. on a ride
in a wheelbarrow. Mrs. shivered,
clutching flannel robe, knees tight to chest,
Mr., teeth gritted, shirt untucked, acted
like it was just a walk in the park.
The cowbell serenade was rough enough to wake
the dead. I'm leaving on the afternoon
train the day we get married.

Wedding Day

I picked June 9 as our wedding day,
same day as my sister
so we could celebrate together.
Took one more year to build my trousseau.
While town accepted Ray's bid to build the library,

I prepared for our wedding.
He planted a backyard garden.
Spring rains left everything lush and green—
peas climbed the back fence,
we picked the pods for our wedding dinner.

Ray spent the morning instructing his men,
arrived at noon, just in time.
Some guests joked he might not appear,
but he did, gallant in a new blue suit.

—*continued*

We stood in an archway facing the guests.
A simple one-ring ceremony
in my parents' living room.
After a few hours of dinner, conversation,
and congratulations,

we snuck out the back kitchen door
for an awaiting taxi to thwart
the larks of merry guests.
They discovered our departure,
following five miles out of town
in a spirited honking of horns.

Our luggage had been wrapped, tied,
and over knotted. We looked
like foreign refugees arriving
at the Peoria railroad station,
but we made it out scot-free
for our Chicago honeymoon.

Mr. and Mrs. George W. Jenike

announce the marriage of their daughter

Marguerite Louise

to

Mr. Ray H. Lillibridge

on Wednesday, the ninth day of June,

Nineteen hundred and fifteen

Delavan, Illinois

The Props Assist the House

—Emily Dickinson

Ray will raise a house
to bind his coming marriage:
A foundation to build a family,
lacking and longed for since young.

To affirm its pattern on the earth,
He marks by snapped chalk cord between stakes,
umbilical cut beneath the prairie's frost line,
support pillars forged of poured cement.

Ray lays down something of himself
into this house, and the earth and wood and stone
give force of their own back into Ray;
life of his household, the center, begins.

Brick by brick the foundation rises, flat flush
sills support thick struts spanning walls.
Ray positions floor joists across these beams,
bracing each, entwined trunks, a tree of life.

Marguerite teaches in a one-room school
two miles out of town, passing daily,
she sees skeleton frame and fireplace
climb, her spirit leavening.

Lumber is stretched straight prior to use,
measured twice, cut once. The frame will hold
its weight, bend but not break, expand in heat,
shrink in cold, keep together as one.

Ray feels the wood's grain. Gauging age and life,
he does not let this spark die, letting live wood
guide his hands and tools, channeling
its spirit into the house as he builds.

Marguerite sees her home boughs thicken,
canopy roof rising toward heaven.
Ray, still yearning, climbs scaffolding,
nailing a cottonwood branch on the peak.

They toast with sweet cider, crisp
tang of ripe apples fresh off the tree.
Hand in hand they climb the stairs,
cross the porch to the front door.

Wedding Portraits of Ray and Marguerite Lillibridge, 1915

Marguerite Lillibridge, 1920

First Home-Cooked Meal

Ray moved us in June 21, 1915,
and I was to fix our first meal.
How I worked. I had every recipe card out,
notes on everything written down,
so I would know what to do. I asked Ray,
"What would you like to eat?"

He'd been used to Mama's best,
"Let's just have bacon and eggs."
So bacon and eggs it was.
And strawberry shortcake, which mother made
with soft strawberries from our garden,
rose-red, to this day makes my lips tingle.

Mother left because she thought
we should have our first meal alone.
I thought so too, but Rita Allen came
over that Sunday afternoon, and we
waited 'til she went home to have supper,
because I'll be darned—I wasn't going

to have a guest for our first meal.

From the *Delavan Tri-County Times*

December 30, 1915, a white Christmas.
Snow started falling the morning before,
fell all day long and well into Christmas Eve,
the ground covered twelve inches deep.

All trains late Christmas Eve,
Christmas Day, clear with a bright mantle of snow.
Sleighing and coasting revived,
but sleighs have not entirely ousted
the autos, for the latter flounder

through the snow in search of traction,
like pigs deep in mud.
Monday morning, coldest of the season
thermometer registering as low as six below zero:
we snuggle around the fire.

Marguerite's *Tannenbaum*

I remember with delight, early Christmas
morning, my father coming to wake me,
carrying me downstairs. As we turned
the corner, I saw a breathtaking sight:
a tree lit with what seemed a hundred candles.

It was a German custom—few families
had Christmas trees. We always did,
whether there were presents around it—or not.

Mother's delicate hanging lamp
had crystal prisms that sent
the lights of the tree
in rainbows across the room,
our house scented pine, like a fairy forest.

One Christmas, I wanted a doll,
Mama's family came,
I slept with my parents in the dining
room, around a stove with isinglass
windows, gleaming, green, purple, red.

When I awoke in the morning, it wasn't
the Christmas tree I saw,
but by my little bed roll,
set a darling baby doll and a buggy,
special to me, as a Rolls Royce.

Hogging Catfish

> *Under fallin' trees, the catfish stay,*
> *dreamin' in water muddy*
> *till I tickle their belly.*
> *Wake up*
> *Hog Wallace wants to play.*
>
> —William Hog Wallace

You boys are telling a whale of a tale.
Came out lame, even you don't believe it.
I met Wallace once years ago. He was
a man just like you and me, even if
he's as famous as Paul Bunyan. His
mind reckoned like a fish, knew what
the fish was thinking before the fish did.
In one day he taught me more than you'll ever
learn in a lifetime on the Mackinaw.

Look, catfish have their home in sunken holes,
you need to go down into their haunt
and tickle them just right. When they feel
comfortable with you bein' there,
sneak your left hand up into their mouth
like to kiss 'em. They'll wake up in a tizzy
realizin' you ain't their mama catfish,
sweating bullets to get out of that hole
they're in. Expect that fish to reflex
jerk forward and chomp on your hand.

This gives you a fighting chance.
Noodle your right hand into their gills,
hold on tight while you grunt him out
of the water. This can be a real dogfight.
Old river cat wants to go down deep,

make you bottom feed. Take a big gulp
of air and hoist 'em out, up on the bank.
Out of water, you'll win, but if you follow
them down to the bottom of the barrel,
catfish wins. You may never resurface.

I got mighty cocky after Hoggin'
a few river cat over the years.
I forgot what my pappy told me 'bout
danger under water. Sometimes a beaver
or 'gator can be in that catfish hole.
Sometimes a loggerhead cooter is lurking
below. One day when I reached down
to tickle a catfish, snap, snap, crunch, a big old
snapper bit on my hand, its beak sharp

as metal snips. Got me a four-fingered
left hand. Now I test catfish holes with
a hickory stick, before I tickle
that cat. Old snapper turtle don't like
to let go, after he bites on a stick.

Let's drive to the Mac this weekend
Ray. Teach us to Hog Catfish?
Must be hard working carpentry
minus a finger?

Not at all, I replied, straightening
my bent finger. *Like I said, boys, when you*

tell a whopper, say it like you believe it.

Saturday Ritual

My Granddad was a cobbler.
We each owned two pairs of shoes,
Sunday shoes and everyday shoes.
When our Sunday shoes got worn
they became our everyday shoes.

On Saturday we'd line shoes up on newspaper
on the long wooden seat in the bay window
apply black or brown polish with a felt
brush and rub them with a cloth until
they were spit-shiny for Sunday school.

When my brother and sisters weren't looking
I tried to move my shoes onto
the newspaper's funnies so I could read
The Katzenjammer Kids
while I shined my shoes.

Saturday was bath day, we'd all have a bath
starting with the oldest and working down
to younger ones in the newest and largest
tub in town. The young ones always soaped
and slid down the tub splashing the others,

in the biggest bathtub in all of Delavan.
They had to delay moving into the house
until the plumbing was in. Ray brought
Grams over to see the bathroom, said,
Etsie, Dad's name for Grams,

You are going to be the first one
taking a bath in this tub. She loved it,
not having a bathroom in her house.
And soon, Saturday afternoons,
the whole family came—for bath day.

Ray Lillibridge Jr. and Ruth Lillibridge Hall, 1922

Main Street Saturday Night

We each were given a dime on Saturday
opening a universe of possibilities.
All the stores stayed open and people
flocked into town. Mr. and Mrs. Reynolds
set up a popcorn stand on Reinheimer's
corner and soon after lighting a little stove,
sounding like small firecrackers, popping began.

A lovely aroma floated over Main Street,
luring the crowd closer, and ever closer,
enticing, craving, hot popcorn in brown paper bags
slathered with butter and a touch of salt.
A regular for five cents and a big bag for ten.
Just got to have it, like a hankering
for pickles and ice cream when pregnant.

We were sorely tempted, even though it would mean
no big scoop of peanuts from the huge
barrel keg at Mike Laffey's A&P,
no purchase of *guess what* candy
wrapped with a surprise inside,
at Gamber & Roemer's Store,
no ice cream cone from Thom's café—
bonus in the bottom of the cone,
a paper saying, *you won a free*
cone or *better luck next time.*
What a treat it was to walk the length of town
on Saturday night faced with such momentous decisions.

Full and happy, later, we'd saunter up
and down Main Street one or two trips more.
Time slowed down, women shared new
recipes and the price of produce. Dad, laughing
shooting the breeze with a group of farmers,
drinking Coca Cola, finding out if any sheds
needed to be built or barns repaired, discussing the price
of next year's seed, finding out
who's really working, who's *just looking busy.*

The evening passed, finally
someone remembered tomorrow
was church day. Afterwards a big dinner
with the whole family gathered
at one home or another—so they had
best get home to sleep, so not to deny
the cock that crows early in the morning.

There is no object I wouldn't give to relive
my childhood growing up in Delavan—
where everyone knew everyone—
and joy came with but a dime.

Ray and Marguerite Lillibridge with Ray Jr. (left) and Ruth (right), 1918

Chicken Every Sunday

First we children went to Sunday school,
then church, then home for play clothes,
the Sunday funnies, and our
tasks for the big dinner of the week:
Oven baked chicken, sides
of mashed potatoes and giblet gravy,
corn and lima bean succotash,
biscuits, Jell-O, wilted lettuce salad.

At dinner, the youngest got a drumstick,
Mother a wing, Dad the breast. One Sunday,
Alice looked out our breakfast room window
for our chickens, each one named by us kids:
Rusty was a Rock Island Red,
Specks a Plymouth Rock, and Blackie . . .
Alice's chicken, Blackie was missing.
No child consumed chicken that day.

We all ate together, the youngest
child who could say a prayer gave grace.
Had the child had been bad or wished a special request
at the end of the prayer would come,

Lord, let me go to the Circus, or *Forgive*
me for breaking Mom's flower vase.

When Grams Jenike ate Sunday dinner
with us she would give her German grace:

—*continued*

Kom Her Jesu
Se unset gast
Und segna wa die
Uns bescheret hast.

Come, dear Jesus
Be our guest
And bless what you
Have shared with us.

For dessert, homemade rhubarb
pie or cherry pie from our orchard.
Gathering around the table always
special, the needs of all remembered,
no matter the afternoon activities, no one
left the table until everyone was done.

Most Sunday afternoons, Granddad came by
to hear Paul Rader's sermons
on the Atwaller Kent wooden-cabinet, eight-tube radio.
We'd see him, coming up the walk,
with a can of fresh marshmallows:
two for each kid, plus one extra for the first one
to meet him at the door. And we'd run!

Our Sunday Race—
for a marshmallow.

Potatoes in the Bedpan

Sunday at noon, Mother asked Carolyn, six, and Alice,
four, to get potatoes for dinner, from the cool,
dark basement, our fruit room. The girls hated
this task, the basement spooky,
the fruit room far off.

Entering the large middle basement
room, Carolyn spied a bedpan hanging
on a hook. It would hold potatoes perfectly.
Seeing the pan with Sunday dinner's spuds,

Mother was furious and told Dad to punish them.
Dad took the girls into his back bedroom,
asked each to go into his closet and bring
out a shoe. Alice quickly grabbed one of Dad's
heavy work shoes. Carolyn more deliberately
sought through the closet floor for a soft slipper.
The discrepancy between the two shoes made Dad laugh.

Mother and Ruth had their ears
to the door, and heard Dad say forcefully,
Turn over for a whipping.

Behind the door Dad whispered,
Holler like a bat out of Hades.
Instead of using the heavy shoe,
he clapped his hands together loudly.

Clap—Alice cried out, *Ouch*;
Clap—Alice bawled, *Oh argh,* blubbering;
Clap—Carolyn, practicing for her later life
in theatre — lamented, *Why me, hateful life?*

First Day of School

First day of school, always a rush.
We crossed the Third Street railroad bridge
stopping at Dad's wood shop until the school's
tower bell rang a warning class was about to start.

The grade school janitor, Bun Day,
kept the lawn pristine, calling it his
Sunday grass. All the children stayed
on the sidewalk in front of the school

never set foot on Bun's Sunday grass.
Bun would often delay ringing
the final tardy bell until
the last Lillibridge kid raced in.

Behind the school, was our play yard--
a merry-go-round, swings, and a landing patch
of grass where the big metal tubes leading down
from the second floor, deposited children in case of fire . . .

The teacher's desk sprouted a row of shining
red apples. All our eyes were fixed
on the chalkboard, waiting on our teacher's
every word with sporadic attention,

even Miss Rumble, a fire-eating redhead,
who once chased a boy around class
with a ruler. He jumped in a tube,
as she neared, zoomed down, free!

Delavan Grade School 1871–1964

Monday Wash Day

No washers and dryers in those days—
we had a scrub board with brass ridges.
In the basement sink, we soaked
clothes in hot soapy water, our
soap homemade from lye,

bacon drippings and rainwater. Often
we had to scrub and scrub to get out sweat
and dirt, sometimes a collar,
cut off, turned over and sewn back:
no ring around the collar was allowed.

Baby's diapers were dropped
in a huge pot of boiling water
atop the basement's little cast iron stove,
then brought over with a wood stick to scrub.
Clothes, pushed by hand through a ringer to squeeze

out water again and again after rinsing.
Seems we always had a big wash
to do. In winter, a wicker basket full
of clothes, wet and clean,
was hung in the basement,

in Spring, neighbors vied to see
who'd be first to hang their wash outside.
Sometimes Mother'd have us run
to put clean clothes out on the line

just to win the Monday Wash Day Olympics.

Ironing Tuesday

Says the old rhyme: Monday washing,
Tuesday ironing, Wednesday sewing,
Thursday marketing, Friday cleaning,
Saturday baking, Sunday go to meeting.

Tuesday everything was ironed:
sheets, pillowcases, handkerchiefs, shirts,
dresses. Thick cast irons stayed
hot on the back of the kitchen
stove, a handle clipped on to use.

We used those irons, even after electricity.
Our second floor had no heat and under covers,
a hot iron wrapped in a towel
kept feet mighty toasty at night.

In the kitchen, Mother ironed Dad's shirts
the older kids helped to make dinner,
while a younger child sat on a stool
reading aloud their first reader.
With seven children, Mother kept
her irons in many fires at once.

Market Day

Jim Pittsford's grocery
smelled of bananas ripening
and the coffee he ground by hand,
wonderful smoked ham and bacon fresh sliced.
He'd reward the child
who came to pick up the purchase,
with a large dill pickle
and always saved the best for us.

The bike ride to Plut's Bakery a treat:
nose lifts, head turns, hypnotized,
by the morning aromas of warm bread,
just out of the oven,
and wrapped in wax paper, before 9 am.
Our family favorite, their long frosted
cinnamon rolls, eight for 20 cents.

J B Foot grew a huge garden,
pushed a two wheeled cart
full of fresh vegetables and summer fruit
down the street, ringing a big bell
calling, *Sweet corn ten cents a dozen.*

Sundays, J B sat in the back pew
east side of the Presbyterian Church.
One day he quit going.
Took offence—
when the new minister
stopped using King James
version of the bible.

Biking home, skillfully balancing Jim Pittsford's bacon,
J B's tomatoes and peaches, while sniffing a
tantalizing spice rising from fresh warm rolls,
I nibbled my pickle reward.

Ruth's First Business, Age Eight

I was in second grade
when older brother Ray
set up Dad's surveying equipment,
looked out through it.

What are you doing?
Getting a look at those guys camped out at the railyards . . .

Through the tripod magnifying glass
we saw close up how the hoboes lived
down near the tracks. This gave me an idea.

Ray and his buddies went down
to the brickyard pond to swim,
I set up the tripod in our back porch,
announced to the neighborhood girls
for five hair pins or one barrette,
I'd let them look.

Soon Mother's purple felt pincushion
was full of pins.
What a successful first business venture!

Imagine their chagrin,
Ray and his buddies
skinny-dipping:
caught!

Coca-Cola Girl

Alice gazed up at the gleaming red
Presto-Speedo bicycle in the window.
Dad told her she could either get a bike
or have a birthday party.

Saturday night in town, impulsively
she grabbed his hand, led Dad
to the window. He had thought
a used bike, painted red, would do.

Noon on her birthday, Alice announced
she'd invited everyone,
even Bill, for a party that afternoon.
All—including her entire third grade class,

her teacher, and on the way to school
she called out for Bill to come.
Bill, an old man of fifty or so,
always sat in front of the Armory

calling out to passing kids
Want some candy?
Mother told us never to speak to him,
just walk past on the other side of the street.

We made rhyming place cards
Mother baked a fortune cake
pale yellow icing, lemon drops round rim,
hidden within treasures,

a ring—you'll be married,
a button—stay a bachelor,
a thimble—always a spinster,
and a penny—you're rich.

After cake, games of Red Light Green Light
and Red Rover, in the play yard.
Fastest prep for a birthday party ever.
Bill did not come. In the garage,

Dad had hidden the red two-wheeler.
Folks still talk of Alice riding that
Presto-Speedo Bike for years around town,
long auburn hair streaming behind her

like a model on a billboard advertisement.
They say she was the Coca-Cola girl.

Aunt Barb

Even on a summer day she'd be wearing
a thick fur coat. She'd offer a love sip
of tea-n-honey on a spoon—lick it off
with a one toothed grin.

She made us take a blood oath:
If you think I'm dead cut off my big toe,
make sure I'm gone. If I wake screaming
like a banshee, no digger man can bury me.

Sometimes, late evening, gnarled hands
mimed up a cyclone, eyes gleaming fire,
she'd chant ancient rhymes from her horsehair
couch. Our eyes lit up to fathom

an uncounted world beyond our ken,
tales of goblins, ghosts and spooks that go "boo"
in the night. Aunt Barb chanted of a *boy*
who never said his prayers, a girl

who sassed her kin, both were plucked away,
fed nothing, save moldy crusts of bread.
And the shaggy man will snatch you
out of nightmare, if you carry on like them.

Behind her out the window, clouds swirled
maniacally, our spine-chilled hairs stood on end,
as a black hole formed in the sky—smoke
luring me away to a stark Stygian void,

till a green cheese moon, rose thru the trees,
like a beacon in primordial chaos.
Her one tooth wobbled, as laughing
she shooed us upstairs for a *sleep*

chock-full-o-dreams. Branches rubbing on the window,
shaggy man's claws mauling at
the bedroom door. I'm alone and quivering
in the dark, praying sleep will never come.

Hoarding

What a treat!
Dad brought home
a bag of potato chips.

We never had such store-bought food!

Dividing up the bag
most of us kids
gobbled 'em up.

I sat on the sunny window seat
slowly savoring chip
after chip
licking my lips
basking in the salty tang.

The others forced to watch.

Dad walked by,
grabbed all of my nest egg,
popped every chip
into his mouth, mumbling,

Aren't these good?

Ruth Lillibridge, August 6, 1946

Thieving

Kids entered Grams Jenike's house
on Pine Street—the one granddad built,
from the back porch,
savoring scents of cooling
pies in a cabinet. Near the pie safe
stood Grams's famous sauerkraut
filling a huge dark brown jar.

Garden cabbage sliced fine, brined with salt,
caraway seeds, studded with juniper berries,

covered by an upside-down plate,
weighed down with two red bricks
sealing a clean flower sack,
atop a few large cabbage leaves
til the 'kraut in the jar fermented.

Each time visiting,
Ruth ducked under the kitchen window,
so Grams would not see, silently creeping
up the steps of the back porch, uncovering
everything:

bricks, plate, flower sack, leaves.

A pleasant sour vinegar scent rising . . .

as Grams watched Ruth
reach in the jar.

Grams

One month old,
brought by her parents to town
in a stagecoach,
household goods following
in a covered wagon.

Paralyzed in a fall,
her father died two years later—
her mother left
alone to raise five daughters.

With determination
the family stayed together.
Caroline married George at nineteen,
a man of German stock

whose grandfather, it's said, served
in Napoleon's Old Guard.
Premature twins followed
a year later, each weighing less

than four pounds, a wedding ring
fit over their hands, tin cups
could slide atop their heads.
Six years later Marguerite was born.

Grams's home stayed open for all,
especially the young folk, relishing
her sweet tea and coffee cake.
The rumor goes, during the Great

—continued

Depression, vagrants marked
her address on the wall in the old
town jail, as a place where no one
was ever refused a free meal,

no matter how many showed up at her door.
Mornings, she often studied with her friend,
a graduate of Howard University,
they read and reread the entire Bible.

In her old age, Grams insisted
on being baptized
again—
by full immersion.

Grams planted pea pods on the fence line
when the moon was full. Whether moved
by tidal forces or her green thumb,
the peas always flourished.

Harvesting sassafras root with Grams
seemed a sacred ceremony.
We'd dig down, take just a little
bit, so each tree would not be harmed.

She cooked from scratch with a pinch of this
and a tad of that.
Selling baked goods helped her
get by, after the bank failed.

For Angel Food Cake,
sift flower seven times
whip twelve egg whites fluffy,
folding in sugar a little at a time
until mix will stick to the dough board
when turned upside down.

The secret, Grams confided
in her nineties, to Jamie age five:
using a finger, scrape out
each shell reclaiming enough
egg white as if adding a thirteenth egg.
That makes all the difference!

I still remember Grams today,
and every time,
breaking eggs for omelets,
I'll wipe the white out of the shells.

Grama Jemnike, Marguerite Lillibridge's Mother

Thunder and Mrs. Hickey

When there was thunder, there was Mrs. Hickey.
When there was lightning, there was Mrs. Hickey.
When a tornado approached, all hell
broke loose with little Mrs. Hickey.

The Hickeys, all very short of stature, lived next door.

Mrs. Hickey had straight gray hair, little
spectacles, a round pudgy face and stood
hardly four-foot-high wearing boots.

Long straight dresses cascaded down to her feet.
Her feet didn't walk forward or backward,
but straddled sideways,
wobbled left, wobbled right,
moving forward like a duck,
gaining ground inch by inch. The umbrella
covered three quarters of her body,

but we all knew it was Mrs. Hickey.

Profoundly afraid of temperature changes,
she would shudder and come
unannounced to our front porch
with the slightest overcast sky—
we could predict the weather by her arrival.

Mother was undaunted by any indication
of a sunny day turning into the wrath of God.

We children would congregate on the porch
during thunderstorms. Mother would say,
That's God moving the furniture around.

With each billowing thunder, we would guess
which piece of furniture God was moving—
a big sofa or a child's chair?

Once a truck pulled up at the house
wanting to know where Dad was
and if we had any canvas roofing canopies at home.
The storm had taken off roofs on the west end of town.
Mrs. Hickey bobbled in a tizzy, dancing around,
telling us kids to hide inside.

We figured with all that ruckus,
someone was moving a whole town in heaven.

Mrs. Stewart

lived directly across the street
in a white frame house.

Ten years older than Dad,
Mrs. Stewart was a kleptomaniac.

Grocery owners were on the lookout
when she entered their stores.

Often she would have a banana, or an apple,
or even a jar of marmalade hidden

in her apron dress. None of our family
ever visited the Stewarts,

but she frequently came over,
entering our living room and staying

until the spirit moved her to go home.
Mother told me she often took things—

that it was a bad habit she had—
I should keep both eyes on her all the time.

Mother could not waste her whole day visiting,
but she was kind to Mrs. Stewart.

Whenever Mother left the living room
to do washing,

ironing, or fix dinner,
she would say to me,

honey, you have a good visit
with Mrs. Stewart.

Prairie Fire

It's been hotter than a cob stove.
No matter how many times I dip a rag
in the well, tuck it under my hat,
still feels like I'm sweating flames.

Sleeping outside every night,
only way you can cool down round here.
Tomorrow I'm gonna start framing
the rafters. In a couple more days

it'll look like a house. We're lucky
anything still remains. One week ago
the hinges of purgatory came unglued.
Up the hill the tall grass began to shake,

with the buzz of a thousand
rattlers of fire struck down at us.
Wildfire fast as a bull
seeing red and snorting steam.

We stopped work and fought the blaze
with wet sacks and prayers for breath.
A touchy time for a while, one of the biggest fires
I've ever seen, took out the old house,

several haystacks and two hundred acres
of pasture sleek and clean.
We saved the barn, and
new foundation.

Hot just ain't the word,
It was the pits of Hades.

II

Sun and Air

where the sky begins
high as a tart chokecherry
rooted twice as deep

Time to Thresh

Wheat and oats turn fields
pale gold every year
by July 4th—
it's time.

Grain is cut and bunched in bundles,
the bundles tied with twine,
twelve bundles make
a shock.

Stand sheaves heads up to dry.
If knocked down by summer storms,
stack them up
again.

When the sheaves are dried, bring hayracks,
pitch bundles on the racks,
take filled wagons
to the barn.

A steam tractor powers the thresher,
spins the canvas belt;
we pitch grain bundles
in.

Chugaaa, chugaa, chuga, faster,
belt turning, hiss, whirling,
steam rising—
blows whistle.

Threshed grain pours into the wagon,
straw shoots onto ground,
oats put into bin
for feed.

Wheat, cash crop, goes to elevator,
Straw, wrapped in twine
bales, saved for
bedding.

Back at the farmhouse, the women pump water,
fill clay jugs, cover with wet burlap
to keep water
cool.

Bring jugs out by horse and buggy.
Unharness work horses at noon
for water
and rest.

Stinging horseflies bite—all jump.
Men wrap fresh ice chunks in bandannas,
tuck inside
their felt hats.

Amazing how much heat you can stand,
when your head is cool!
Sweaty shirts dry —sun
ironed.

—*continued*

Neighbors help each other,
going farm to farm to thresh,
two days: fifteen
acres.

Bring a dish
for the midday potluck—big
appetites after
hot work.
Delicious feast!
Strawberry rhubarb pie
fried chicken, all
the fix'ns.

Ah, the smell of fresh baked biscuits,
creamy butter fresh off
the churn, and cool
sweet tea.

After all fields are harvested, a big picnic,
down by the Mackinaw river. The best part,
swinging on a rope
tied to a tree,

landing far out in cool water.

Chet Inskip

lanky, fiftyish, ungainly, wore his revolver
on a hip, big silver belt buckle
on his lower middle.
Walked like a bucking bronco rider
just jilted off the bull,
mighty proud to be chief of police.

Widow Mrs. Hart was the opposite:
overly manicured, starched white collar,
gloves, tiny brimmed hat.
An odd couple when the two walked
down Main Street
hand in hand.

Each Christmas season, the town stood an enormous pine
in the main street's center, festooned
with lights and baubles, finished with a black top hat.
Saturday before, Santa and sleigh appeared,
bearing bags of candy for,
us good boys and girls.

One Christmas advertised an extra feature—
Santa was bringing Mrs. Claus.
Sure enough, Mrs. was there at his side
in a red dress, white hair askew,
spiked through a burgundy and lace hat,
robe dismantled, on close examination

brown chewing tobacco flowed
from Mrs. Claus's mouth.
We could see
Mrs. Claus was Chet Inskip,
but the bag of candy he handed out
was still delicious.

Decoration Day

It's a long walk up the hill on Sundays,
but peaceful to sit with you, Son.

Today's a bit more festive,
the peonies unfurl, Mom's loaded down
with flowers: bleeding hearts, phlox, ferns, and poppies.
Arrived early for the parade and found

Prairie Rest Cemetery bedecked with flags,
Stars and Stripes on poles up and down the drive,
and flowers, flowers everywhere,
people wearing poppies, decorating

graves of kin, some still hoping
for returning soldiers. Marching in they came,
William Hobson hobbling in the lead,
Delavan's last survivor of the Civil War.

All stood in honor to salute, or place a hand
across their hearts. Spanish-American War
vets followed, and your platoon from World War I.
Taps played first in Prairie Rest, and echoed

from a cornfield nearby.
There wasn't an eye stayed dry.
Scouts led the pledge of allegiance, followed by
Ray junior reciting The Gettysburg Address:

that these dead shall not have died in vain—
that government of the people, by the people,
for the people, shall not perish from the earth.
Marguerite's tearing eyes shone proud.

Things break'n up now, another Decoration
Day is done. It's empty at home without you,
Son. Next Sunday Mom and I will return to sit
a spell, after the long walk back up the hill.

Posting the Ice Card

in our front window
lets Ike Diekhoff know how much
ice we need

ice pick breaks chunks off block
we rush to his truck for a sliver
of summer's delight

fresh milk, in a glass bottle
our dairyman delivered
each morning, and

jars of farm butter,
flowers and fresh herbs
pressed on the top

ice cream's best when homemade,
cream, sugar, salt, crushed ice
endless hand cranking

I'll do the first hundred
turns, if you do the next fifty—
thick cream's hard to crank

lazy days on the porch
eatin' peppermint ice cream
each bite, July's fireworks.

Orange Crate Scooter

Like my Dad
I'm handy with a hammer
screwed roller skates
on a two-foot board
hammered an orange crate
braced at a slight angle
old bike handlebars on top—

Orange Crate Scooter born.

Riding down third street into town
the concrete's grooved
before the railroad bridge.
Wheels boom over grooves
bass echoes off the Orange Crate's slats

wakes up hoboes,
gets stray dogs to barking.

Over the bridge and down the hill
past the new Armory, leaning
into the turn
                                        wheels screeching
bunny hop UP
                    pulling with all your might
                    on the handlebars

barely clearing the curb
                                        brake hard
at Dad's workshop.

Repeat one hundred times
till perfect.

Black Thursday

At the dining table,
Dad says softly, *Well Carolyn,*
there goes your grand piano,
Ruth, bye bye college education.

Til now Delavan had two banks.
Baldwin Bank fails:
Grams and Gramps Jenike lose all their money.
No withdrawals from Tazwell County Bank,
until FDR gives his *Nothing to fear*
but fear itself speech.
The Great Depression sets in.

Dad buys Grams and Gramps a new furnace.

Two gardens, a big strawberry bed,
keep our table full:
rows of string beans, beets,
corn, carrots, peas, cucumber hills,
four apple trees, two cherry trees,
two grape arbors, white and red.

Flyer wagon filled
with surplus, we kids sell door to door.
Mother told us
give a baker's dozen—
always plus one.

Mrs. Morris would strip
every ear of corn,
and not buy any.
Hildreth Sowa pinches each tomato,
wants a discount for bruises.

No financial security,
not for anyone, though
Dad keeps detailed books,
expenses everything,
nails to shingles.

No money to build houses.
If barns and silos need repair,
folks try to fix it themselves,
before hiring Dad, then asking
him to put their bills *on the books*.

Lena Slack

talked like a parrot, moved like a jaguar
acted like a vulture.

All the kids hated her.
she reciprocated.

When something went wrong at her home
she blamed us Lillibridge kids.

Halloween, a posse of high school boys
turned over nearly every privy in town,

flipped Lena Slack's outhouse
threw ripe tomatoes

on her freshly painted front porch.
Lunch hour, Daniel Cheever, Delavan High School principal
made the entire class

go round restoring privies right side up
scrub each porch clean.

Not good enough:

Lena's evil vulture eyes
willed them all stone dead.

Hank Pree

turned over his own mother's privy,
along with everyone else's. No one would
guess he was a Halloween prankster.
Principal Cheever wasn't fooled.
Hank too was punished
with restoration clean-up.

Hank was an excellent drummer.
Undertaker Houghton
befriended him, let him keep his drums
at the Funeral Parlor on Main Street.
We'd go after school.

Putting on a 78 RPM record,
Hank closed the drapes
and played along with his drums.
A corpse in the back room,
we would dance and dance.

Our parents found out,
and funeral parlor dancing ceased.
Irate church moms:
Dancing! Act of the Devil!
Somber and composed,

funeral director Houghton
softly agreed, *Be respectful
of the dead.* Then winked.
*If only you'd been playing
When the Saints Come Marching In.*

When Jazz Became Swing

Bribed with candy bars,
shades pulled down,
"Stardust" on the turntable.
Ray trained his little sisters
before school tea dances
to jitterbug and swing.

Ray conducted the Lucky Strikes Hit Parade
on the radio with his baton,
could play Moon Indigo's
solo on his clarinet, transpose music
for each instrument in his band.
Practice sessions jammed in our home,
a solid beat with a strong dance groove.

Minister Starr Beatty preached
The Evils of Dancing! Jezebels!
Temptation of the Devil!
never knew his son
was the one gathering signatures
to endorse our high school dance.

My mother: one of the first to sign.

It was the time of
Wayne King, Artie Shaw,
Big Band Music.
We danced the Big Apple—
couples formed a ring
Suzie Q left, Suzie Q right,
counterclockwise circling,

arms held high.

Division of Labor

The evening meal done,
Ruth would wash the dinner dishes,
Carolyn, dry.

Week after, the jobs would switch.
Ruth, scheduled to dry, had a date.
Carolyn, no date,
took her time washing.

Ruth's date
sat on the front porch,
waiting and waiting.
Ruth, fit to be tied.

Sisters' screaming heard
all the way
down to the railroad bridge!

Dad solved this.

If the washer
did not have the dishes washed
before the dryer's date arrived,

dishwasher would have to wash and
dry.

Stray

Tramps slept under the third street railroad bridge,
washed in the brickyard pond,
Depression made times hard for us all.
Still, Mother would bring them sandwiches—
got mad finding
the bread discarded, only the meat eaten.

Stray dogs hung out under the bridge.
One came out to greet me,
scruffy looking, reddish-brown mane.
I brought him treats. He began
trailing me to school,
waiting after

to follow me home.
Tagging behind me to the brickyard,
he'd guard my clothes
while I swam in the pond.

Dad pointed out the breakfast room
window, *Whose dog is that Jim?*

Just a stray that adopted me.

Dad went outside, walked around the dog,
tilting up his head, looking a long
time—one eye brown, one eye blue.

Can we keep him... please?
I'll call him Rusty.

Dad found a beat-up metal dish.
This dog will be your true friend,
always remember his needs.
Never let this dish be empty. Winter
or summer, always keep it full of water.

Dad swallowed hard.
Rusty it is.

Sister's Oath

Sitting 'round the kitchen table
sisters made a pact:
not to be the first to wed.

First Carolyn, and 'round the table,
each, in turn, pledged
not to split their close family.

Alice fell in love, married Dean in 1945.
Looked everywhere at the reception,
found Dad alone in the back bedroom.

He admitted being a little sad,
If you have to marry, Dean is the perfect choice.
Ray loved having all his daughters close.

The couple made the trip home,
Dad's last Christmas, traveling
from Oak Ridge, Tennessee,

where Dean was stationed,
security on the Manhattan Project.
Dad slipped Alice a note,

A long trip just to spend two days
with your old man,
best Xmas present I could get.

Teaching himself Spanish from
a book, wrote, *Cada uno*
in su casa y Dios in la de todo.

Each one in his house and all in God.

Lillibridge children at Donna Lillibridge's wedding in the Lillibridge House (left to right) Alice, Ray Jr., Donna, Mary, Ruth, and Carolyn, with Jim Lillibridge in the foreground

(backrow, from left) Ray Jr., Carolyn, Donna, Ruth, Alice
(sitting, from left) Marguerite, Mary, Jimmy, Ray,
and Rusty the dog, with the Lillibridge house in the background, 1942

Holiday Card 1942

Merry . . . the letters began to form—
Ruth's pen poised in midair
over a Christmas Card.

Can anyone be merry this year?

half the world using tears for Christmas baubles,
enough misery to fill a lake.

The world is not Merry, when we forget the needs of others.

What words can sing out
over the shouts of war . . .
echoes of pain . . .
and bitter isolation?

There is but one thought,
a message of tenderness,
reassurance,
the everlastingness of God's love.

Merry Christmas!

Marguerite Mourns

Won't be the same Thanksgiving
this year or ever. There never was
another man quite as fine or good.

It seems Dad is here now.

Everything breathes his presence.
I am contented being home around
things he loved so much. I have his
old blue sweater, like having a part of him.

I should hear his step, his chuckle,
Margaret, where's the matches?
my pen and ink? I sense soon he'll
come down the drive in his old truck.

I want him close. I should be grateful
I had him through all those dreadful war years.
He'd been so sick that one winter.
I guess God's especially kind

to us after all. We are fortunate,
having a large family,
more to share in happiness,
more to share in sorrow.

Center of the World

A small house, on a quiet street,
in a small town, built a century ago.
Nestled among farms
tilling the rich dark soil,
eons of prairie grasses laid down,
returning a bounty of grain,
helping to feed the world.

Womb where dreams are made,
place where the past, and thoughts
beyond remote memory of the past,
awaken from shadow. Deep
within us a truth,
a genuine state of mind,
where childhood is affirmed.

Huddled in blankets in the unheated
upstairs bedroom, nearer the open sky,
between heaven and earth, the abode
of those who believe. Fifty years ago
it was, and now still in reverie,
a refuge, where children
await Santa every Christmas Eve.

Peering out hopefully at the snow-
blanketed roof, listening intently
for sleigh bells, succumbing
at last to the land of nod. Tomorrow
will bring family and joy.
A small house, once upon a time,
the center of our world.

Offspring Anthropologists

Marguerite, now Nanya, raised seven children
between these walls. Now unoccupied,
lamps keep watch, awaiting their return.
Ancient mirrors on dresser tops,
their dim luster— spirits in amber light,
ancestors welcoming the young.

Decals on the glass window
of the upstairs bedroom door celebrate
Big Ten football teams in the 1930s,
the time Red Grange played
for the University of Illinois.
Toys and books remain, hidden treasures

stuff wardrobes: a box of original Lincoln
Logs, tinker toys and marbles
multicolored and sized,
locked diary without a key, old
copper pennies larger than a quarter,
wooden puzzles, from yesteryear, all

waiting for a child to rediscover.
Subterranean forces, dark
entities below the house require
exploration—but not alone.
Individuals might never return.
Each room in the labyrinth holds wonders.

Here, our grandmother, Nanya,
ran the Hobbyhorse Kindergarten
after husband Ray died.
Scouting out the cloakroom—
deciphering the mystery
of coat hook names.

Margie and Bob are cousins.
Who is Kate? The big room
set with small tables and chairs.
A hand-printed poster of Pogo
Possum and Porky Pine, cartoon characters
from the 1940s, look down over a large

chalkboard, handmade by my grandfather
for his girl Marguerite,
when she taught in a one-room
country school. Later, Ray gone,
school closing, Nanya purchased
chalkboards to use again.

In a side room, called The Bar 20 Corral,
cowboy boots, spurs, carved, painted
wooden horseheads attached to poles
adorn the walls waiting to be taken
out for ridin'
in the play yard out back.

My grandfather, a fan of Hopalong
Cassidy, clean cut, sarsaparilla-drinking
hero from the Bar 20 ranch.
Brought up in South Dakota in the 1800s,
Ray would have been a cowboy
if life had not gotten in the way.

Deeper still, darkness prevails,
unlit rooms filled with cobwebs,
moldy wardrobes, rusting cast iron
beds, a large wicker baby carriage,
an ancient Victrola.
Farther beyond, a space entered

—continued

only by an expedition made up of
those truly brave, probing
diabolical depths of the root cellar.
Floor damp, perhaps due to an immense, black,
stagnant body of water beneath.
Illuminated only by a faint

phosphorescence reflecting off jars
of decomposing vegetables, some
cracked and oozing slime,
this chamber hints at
deep alchemical meaning,
transformation for future discovery,

when our courage improves.
Here on the wall hangs a metal bedpan
peeling white-stained enamel,
never to be touched.
Legends utter dire punishment
for breaking this solemn taboo.

Who of sound mind would ever touch a bedpan?

May Basket

The doorbell rang. I opened it.
On the step lay an orange
crepe-paper basket
filled with popcorn,
jellybeans, and flowers.
I saw Jenny waving across the street.
I gave chase.

She was a year older,
longer-legged, faster.
Nevertheless,
soon I caught her.
Auburn hair brushed my face,
whiffs of bluebells and baby's breath,
fleeting spring blossoms.

I smiled a sheepish
grin, thanked her,
retreated home.
She looked a little disappointed.
Forty years later, I reminisce:
I lost my chance to dance around the maypole,
my chance to steal a kiss.

Prairie Pixies

The play yard sparkles,
lit by dancing fairies at dusk.
The moon, colored rose, rising over
the water tower's dark silhouette,
reveals a land of brindled magic.

Quick jibe leeward,
I'm heeling over, rising,
summer's warmth fills me,
sailing to chart the vast Milky Way.

Ten little fireflies
in the air so high.
Are you elves and pixies
floating in the sky?

Whirling over fields,
dancing on the prairie—
caught in my Ball Jar.
Take me to fairyland, little pixie.
She'll never grant wishes
captured in a jar,
even with nail holes
on top to allow breathing.

If you'll be my lantern,
lighting up the garden night,
I'll let you free
little pixie.

Rocking on the screen
porch, we plan a palace
out of hay bales, to be built
in the barn loft, a castle
riddled with hidden passages,

secret ways only the two of us,
would ever know,
unless Peter Pan
came that night to fly
us to Neverland.

Better let those fireflies
go free, one may
be Tinker Bell.

Time lingers with heads
in the clouds. Legs spring up two
or three stairs at a time,
to the attic bedroom.

Beds were softer then,
we woke day-ready,
dreams, now mere wisps,
too soon lost.

Farm Christmas

Christmas morning
while she is still abed,
Uncle George brings in
a newborn baby piglet,
presents it,
pink and washed
to Ruth's arms.

Aunt Mary's farm breakfast
steams on a long table—homemade
sausage, fresh eggs, thick rich milk,
pastries, pies, dishes of candy
on every table. Pine-scented
candles lit, cousins everywhere!
Glorious bedlam. Huddled

in our bunk beds, swathed under quilted comforters
we speculate —
What is in all the boxes
under the tree? Diabolically,
Bob and I gather, sneak
willow branches upstairs.

We put switches under Jeannie's bed.
She cries. Mother assures
Jeanie, *we'll show*
Beelzebub which bad boys
need coal in their stockings—
and move all of the switches
under our bunk bed.

Thanks, Santa—Bob and I
find electric train sets,
with smoke and lights,
chugging around the tree
Christmas morning—
our fortunes reversed!

(from left) Mary Lillibridge, Jeanie, Jim, and Bob, Christmas 1970

Mother's Day on the Farm

Wake Bob at dawn.
Warm under covers, he
resists sneaking away.
We have work to do,
a creek to dam,
a swimming hole to make.

Stripped down to underwear
we balance driftwood across the banks
mortar with rocks and brush and mud.
The water level begins to rise.
Soon we'll have
a glorious swimming hole.

The power of water is tough
for two ten-year-olds to overcome.
One by one dam sections begin to fail,
plugging hole after hole with mud,
small waterfalls in breaches,
omens of eventual total collapse.

Climbing out of the cavernous creek
between rows of newly planted corn,
craving a farm breakfast, we walk,
devising our triumphant return.
We'll bring lumber off the wood pile
to rebuild our Hoover Dam.

Bob's dad meets us. Hands
on hips, face burning.
We've been gone all morning.
Mothers are up in arms,
ready to call the authorities,
organize a search,
dredge the creek.

Shooed ahead, I hear
behind me the smack of a large
callused hand on Bob's bottom.
It should have been me.
I had lured him away,
we'd cut Sunday School.
Somehow we make it
to church that Mother's Day,
The whole congregation snickers—
wet underwear soaked through
my hastily donned dress pants.

One Off the Bucket List

Wendell at seventy-five had heard enough tales
of Hog Wallace, enough songs of the Mackinaw—
what is all this fuss?

On the river he comes clean,
I've never canoed.

You've never canoed the Mackinaw?

Nope, never canoed.

It's summer, not too hot.

Passing under cathedral cottonwoods,
dodging occasional sandbars,
gliding past secluded spots

where pawpaw trees grow atop
hilltops and hazel nuts abound.
Wendell's eyes sparkle,

I always wondered what
the Mackinaw would be like.

Water churns, current gains speed,
ahead a pile of rocks split the river—
we choose the right-hand fork.

Wrong fork. River narrows,
a slick six-foot-high wall of mud—
the north bank. Brambles and rocks
line the south bank.
Ahead a fallen tree crosses the river,
limbs intertwined
underneath, water roils
forced through a sieve.

We need to back up, take
the other fork, I tell him.

I reckon so, I figured I'd let you
decide, you're the canoe man.

Grabbing a branch delays our descent.

Unable to turn in the tight channel
we paddle backward, current forcing
us against the high mud bank.

Both of us push off with our paddles,
rock to the starboard side,
lean to port.

—continued

Canoe rights
briefly, keeps going, rolls over,
swings past plumb,

upends us into the river.

Enveloped in water
Wendell calls out,
I can't swim.

Into a fulcrum of white water
loose belongings disappear
down the chute, into
a maelstrom beneath
rocks and fallen tree.
Clutching our sodden pirogue

we get to shore.

Free the stuck canoe,
manhandle it up over the steep
slick bank, crawl after,

bellies streaked with mud.

Above the river, we scan its
expanse. Wendell grins,
twinkle in his eye,

Now I've done the Mackinaw.

Old Glory

It's almost winter now. In the air,
I taste snow coming.
Reminds me of the really big snows
of the 1890s. Down from barns and cellars
came the sleds. Father built ours, round steel

runners embedded in solid oak, slits
sawed on the front crossbars for mitten
fingers to fit in and grasp, ready for action.
We painted it red, Old Glory hand printed
gold on its belly, sure to outrun

every sled in town. Facedown, belly tight
to plank, we flew away, ever away.
In those days, Locust Street north of town,
hunkered down with snow,
never plowed, heavy wagon wheel

tracks smoothed out—a bobsled run.
Starting at the top of Library Hill,
bombed past the old brick schoolhouse,
ball diamond, on and on, slowing
to see our competitors on our heels.

—continued

By some strange osmosis, traffic stood still
as Delavan's youth merged on that hill.
The boys in heavy mackintoshes,
wool knickers, knitted caps fit like masks,
openings for mouth and eyes.
Girls protected by a cocoon of wool—
skirts, petticoats, long underwear,

buckled boots. Ned with Flexible Flyer
rushed from West Fourth. Delavan's
baseball stars leapt to their sleds racing.

Annie Lou attacked the hill, laughing
like bells, turned to avoid Eileen
trying a belly buster on wood runner.
Afterwards, starved and soggy,
coasters retired to the Jenike house for hot

chocolate and coffee cake. The smell
of wet wool mittens and scarves drying
by the cookstove. Laughter, and warm drink.
All too soon, it's time to drag sleds home
again, finish work for next day's school.

Old Glory hangs in my garage, paint
stripped, shreds of rope looped through hand slits,
waiting—waiting for the next great-great-
grandchild saying, *Let's take it down.*
Nanya, try her on Library Hill!

Marguerite's Christmas Grace

(Marguerite, age one hundred years, gave these unscripted thoughts transcribed from videotape, at Christmas dinner.)

We thank the Lord that you sent your son
on this blessed day to save us all
and to guide us in the way we should live.

Help us to be more charitable, and kind,
and guide us in what we say and do.

And make this a better world because
we have lived in it.

We thank thee for all the favors, opportunity,
and kindness you have shown us.

We thank you for the family that we had,
and their welcome to us all.

Be with us through the coming years,
And enlarge us in our way of living.

We ask in your blessed name.
Amen.

Margueritte Lillibridge, 1990

Phoenix

Her sun setting in the west, Nanya
rose again with a second childhood.
Enlivened by grandchildren, she rode
grandson Dirk's Kawasaki

1000 motorcycle in her seventies,
sledded down a hill in her eighties
danced a jig Christmas morning
age ninety-nine, with the great-grandchildren.

Marguerite died, family around her,
one hundred years old,
in the house Ray built for their wedding.
A sweet goodbye, passing the torch, teaching us

love is eternal till the end:

Do not grieve,
loss is inevitable.
Love binds us together.
Heaven is much closer now.

III

Green Sod Above, Lie Light

after the deluge
sun's rays wake white sage grass
bind earth and spirits

Margeuritte Lillibridge and Jim Hall (the author)

Walking Back in Time

It's the weekend of Delavan's "house walk,"
and the town decks out for Christmas.
Crowned with a big black top hat,
a Christmas tree towers in the center
of Main Street. One hundred more trees lit

in Veterans Park, honoring our veterans.
For fifty years, Joe Utz, town blacksmith,
attached a huge canvas painting of the nativity
on a downtown building.

Today, the Historical Society's window
displays a section of the original—
the Madonna and Christ child.
Dickens's characters walk the streets.
Watch out for Marley's ghost!

Hundreds of out-of-towners come,
shuttled by carriage to the featured
homes, lit by luminarias.
Hundreds of enslaved folks passed

through Delavan to freedom
on the Underground Railroad. Abraham
Lincoln walked these streets,
working as a circuit lawyer.
The old colony house is open. Its frame

shipped by barge, then wagon from Rhode Island
at Delavan's founding. The library,
built by grandfather Ray, also open.
My mother loves these house walks,
especially when the grand houses on West 3rd

are open. The Crabb house, the Ryan house—
houses her father Ray built.
She holds court telling the current
owners stories of their homes' past.

After touring, we stop at the Presbyterian
Church. Organ music plays upstairs and dinner
is served in the church's basement. We share
dinner with Aunt Donna and Uncle Wendell,

then stop at Aunt Carolyn and Uncle Perry's
for Doreen's cherry pie a la mode,
tales of the night's characters,
how gaudy—or not—the houses.

The An-Teek Shop

across from the library,
better known as the flea market.
A building so rickety you think it will

fall down any second,
lit year-round with Christmas lights,
carrying a hint of mold.

On trips to Delavan,
Jane always stops here.
Catches up on town gossip

from the owner,
tall and lanky,
bug eyed,

balding save one sprouting cowlick—
the grasshopper man.
Gossiping, gossiping, always gossiping.

She picks up hidden treasures,
most
in exchange for social currency.

The Party

The house awakens for Christmas,
and our neighbor Dolly arrives with cookies.
Of course, we are not ready.

How can you prepare for chaos?
Seven children raised in this house
return with their own children, grandchildren,
great-grandchildren, in robust mayhem.

Aunt Alice arrives first with a platter
of shrimp and cocktail sauce, escorted
from Colorado by her daughter Jan.
Family from Tennessee follow through the door.

I take the tenderloin out of the oven,
wrap it in foil to rest, put Jane's macaroni
and three-cheese platter in to cook. On the burner,
steaming Figgy Pudding bursts up out of the pan.

I slip out of the kitchen just in time for the arrival
of the Varneys: storyteller Margie, Alex the epicurean,
Lawyer Bob and his homespun tales,
smiling Jeanie, quick witted Vicki saying,

No one . . . is as funny as you think you are, Bob.
I throw together the punch. One quart of
ginger ale, another of Hawaiian Punch,
a bowl of raspberries and cranberries,
topped off with scoops of pineapple sherbet.

Donna and Wendell come with grandkids
and her Cherry Coke Jello. Dirk and Jill, arms filled
with ready-to-pop popcorn, enter, followed
by Wendy and her clan. The kitchen table fills quickly.

Jane tosses salad in a giant wooden bowl, greets
passing relatives bringing potluck offerings
to table. A hundred years of family
pictures on the wall. I pop a bottle

of champagne to top a cup of punch,
for those so inclined. What am I forgetting?
The keg of homebrewed cider on the porch.
The living room churns with Lillibridges.

Sally and John come, their kids Meg and Perry
loaded down, bearing Doreen's fresh-baked pies.
Aunt Lois for years hosted these gatherings,
now rests comfortably in a chair, a cup of punch in hand.

Outside, the brick walk glows with luminarias.
On the porch, a white Christmas tree with old-fashioned
ornaments, a large plastic Snoopy shining bright.
Gary, Ann, and Carlin come up the sidewalk,

Christmas music, and in the window,
lights strung, star-shaped, twinkle.
In the den, the younger generation
minds the fire—no chestnuts this year.

—*continued*

John and Candy, with their sugar-crazed
Texas kids, chase our German
shepherd Shiloh, who is stalking Isaiah,
egged on by Micah, whooping with glee.

A Christmas tree glows in the den,
another in the living room. Now kept decorated
year-round—their lights lit
only for Christmas. *Dinner is served,* Jane announces.

The clan makes their way through
the kitchen and somehow all find a place
to sit for dinner. Ten around the oak dining
table, six on the bay window's seat,

some perched on living
room couches and chairs, some around the fire
in the den. I was about to sit too,
until I remembered

the pudding.

Plum Pudding

> *The best laid schemes o' Mice an Men Gang*
> *aft agley* [often go askew].
> —Robert Burns

Grams Jenike's recipe: a pinch of this, a dash of that,
steam till done . . . on a woodburning stove.

Trouble crops up translating her recipes into twenty-first century.
My butcher, eyebrows raised, provides the suet.

No plums in plum pudding—
The English call all dried fruit "plums."

Slow cooking needed so suet melts before it expands.
If cooked too fast, the pudding gets hard.

Our simple plan, a flaming show, started flawlessly.
Cousin Jim conducting the clan chorus.

I turn down the burner, steamed pudding bursting
upward like Jiffy Pop popcorn.

Flipped onto plate, pudding separates
easily from the bundt pan, a spotted brown rose.

Splendid! In the dining room, Jim, an entertainment lawyer,
quiets conversations achieving unanimity in song.

—*continued*

We wish you a Merry Christmas,
we wish you a Merry Christmas and a happy New Year!

I take the saucepan of brandy, warming gently on the stove,
and drizzle it generously over the pudding.

In the other room the clan sings louder—
oh, bring us a figgy pudding and a cup of good cheer!

Lights dimmed, I enter the dining room.
With a flourish I present the pudding to the unruly mob.

I touch a long wooden match to it, standing back,
expecting a volcanic explosion. The match burns.

The pudding does not ignite.
I try again, but to no avail.

I can tell I'm losing my audience.
Stammering, I retreat to the kitchen.

my mind races, the porous pudding
must have soaked up all the brandy.

Desperate I light the still-warm pan of brandy.
A small flame of fire glows on the surface.

Reentering the dining room the second chorus ends:
we won't go until we get some, so bring some out here!

I pour flaming brandy over the pudding,
which now ignites according to plan.

A collective sigh echoes through the crowd.
Followed by polite applause.

A small flicker still burns in the saucepan, without
thinking, as if it were a candle, I blow.
A flash of flame erupts over
my face—intense heat and agony!

I again retreat to the kitchen, place
the cover over the still-glowing saucepan,

return red-faced, as if it was all
part of the plan. Pretend not to be in pain.

What's that black smudge above your eye?
Charred eyebrows, now ash, wipe away on my hand.

Hearing sharpened after purification
by fire, snippets of conversation surround me:

There is a lot of brandy in this pudding.
A bite or two later . . .

A lot of brandy!
Can I have another piece?

Legion Hall Sunday Breakfast

Delavan Legion serves breakfast Sunday
mornings 6:30 to 10 am, all welcome.

Under the 3rd Street Bridge
no hoboes here, where once they slept.
The town's stray dogs now snuffle,
scratch for scraps elsewhere.
Even the railroad tracks gone.

The Bridge, famous now—
registered, historic. We walk
from the old home place,
Lillibridge house, me and Jane, our kids,

pass where Ray's shop once stood, now
Jeckel Plumbing, across from the "new" Armory Hall.
Ray purchased the old Armory, took it down,
recycling the massive timbers that once stood watch
over innumerable indoor baseball games.

On the way to the Hall for breakfast,
we pass the imposing cement Armory
that took its place. And later,
when our National Guard disbanded,
was sold
to private owners.

The Vet manning the table welcomes us,
scribbles our order on a notepad,
rips it off with his one good hand.
They've got a system—we get a plastic number,
the cooks get the order, the Legion ladies serve.

Plunk down a few dollars for the lottery —
a stars and stripes quilt we'll never win,
fill our first cup of coffee from an industrial pot.
Row upon row, long tables span the room,

farmers in worn overalls, bikers in worn leather,
girls in T-shirts and yoga pants,
gray hairs everywhere, even a few
of high "tattoo-to-tooth ratio" folks.
Bearing plates of pancakes,

bacon, sausage, farm fresh eggs,
ladies circle the room, call out numbers, bring
breakfast to tables decked with small packets
of jams and syrups. Claire, who worked for Ray

in the forties comes over to greet us.
Gossip envelops us: who is sick,
who passed on, who's gonna buy the distillery,
who will work in Revolution's new
marijuana grow plant east of town.

—*continued*

Wendell and Dirk eat with us—
Cousin Dirk likes a lot of black
pepper on his gravy, Wendell,
prefers his eggs over hard.

Up high, round the room, formal portraits,
past guard commanders hang on the walls.
Over the door to the kitchen, a photo
of Ray junior in uniform, wearing
his bronze star, awarded for service braving enemy fire—
he supplied our boys at Pork Chop Hill.

Spending his final days wheelchair bound,
on constant oxygen,
in the Danville, Illinois, VA hospital,
Ray insisted on attending a Memorial service.
When soldiers marched in with the American flag.
Ray was the first to rise, to salute the colors.

Pictures of others in uniform line these walls,
each with tales of bravery and anguish.
We raise coffee cups aloft,
toast our Delavan heroes.
Time will not fade the glory of their deeds.

Ray Lillibridge Jr.

To a Father Dying Young

inspired by A.E. Houseman

I dreamt of my father last night.
We stand waiting for a table,
in a bustling Italian restaurant.
Aromas of oregano, sage, Chianti
mix with contagious laughter.

The water captain directs servers,
keeps bread baskets filled and tops off wine.
I try to get the maître d's ear,
find out how long until our large party
can be seated. I look across

the room, where Dad is talking
with someone I don't know.
The room is loud. I cannot hear.
Stopping his conversation, he smiles,
sage green eyes penetrate mine,
connect in familiar quiet ease.

A checkered table for two opens.
I think I should grab Dad and take it.
The two of us could sit and reminisce,
but we are part of a group too large to seat.
There will be time to catch up later.

The dream ends before we get a table.
I wake, pillow damp, spent, longing.
So many questions never answered.
Washing sleep from my eyes,
in the mirror, Dad's face looks back at me.

Lowell Hall and Ruth Lillibridge Hall (author's parents), 1945

A Time to Dance

Cemetery ladies,
perfume tinged with formaldehyde,
guard ground with competence and conceit,
keep lists of meetings, costs of plot repairs,
and careful count of those who've died.

They've stripped this resting place—
white oaks downed first, then flaming
maples felled, all shrubbery slashed,
no hallow seen to mar the green,
only plastic flowers they allow,
for death must have no life at all.

Veteran's bronze plaques ordered flat
to the ground. If they rise above one inch,
a lawn machine will grind them down.
They have their rules, clearly stated
on the gate, all who enter here to stay
must mark in stone, both name and date.

Bugle Taps! Let's jazz-rap!
A cry, a call, rising clarion clear,
forget the warnings on the gate,
forget all orders to behave,
come children come, dance on my grave.

Prairie Sunset

inspired by N. Scott Momaday

West of town at sunset,
fields stretch to the far horizon,
the last glowing rays of the day
shimmer on impossibly

straight rows of corn.
Tassels burst, haze of
golden pollen floating,
rising, waiting for the rain.

As long as we keep the Earth, it's true,
She gives us what we need.

The story goes like this:
"Plowing a field the horse stopped,
would not budge, and the boy, Perry,
went to the front to walk him forward.

The nag lunged, and the boy fell.
Sharp sickle steel ran across his leg.
Some power intervened, cutting-
edge catching on a clod of dirt,

the plow popped up and over
his leg, preserving life and limb.
Surviving a century of progress, Perry,
is now buried in Prairie Rest
Cemetery, his tombstone carved,
Green sod above, lie light, lie light.

East of town, clusters of windmills
tower on the prairie, dwarfing
any quixotic passion to resist.

—continued

Where Perry once plowed a field

one row at a time, now satellite-
guided tractors pull thirty-six row,
no-till planters, every field corn seed,
coated with pesticides and fertilizer.

Precision farming,
soil sampling,
moisture sensing,
yield mapping.

Farmer morphs into mechanic,
fixing robot harvesters.

Big data maximizes profit,
shading out the love of dirt.
AI algorithms prevail.
Will they keep the Earth to come?

The Sun in the heartland sets far away,
unscreened by city lights. Through the night's
vibrant stars, a milky sky-river
beacon, rises like a ladder.

Dramatis Personae

Delavan, small town in central Illinois founded in the 1830s, named after a temperance advocate. Over a century ago a House is built here deep rooted in the prairie, the foundation for a family.

Ray, Builder, born in 1881, childhood in Dakotas. Down home humor masked trauma of family broken apart in his youth. As contractor built the town library and many of the stately homes of Delavan.

Marguerite the matriarch, married Ray in 1915, and moved into the home he built for his bride, where she raised a family, lived into her hundredth year, dying in her bed with her family around her.

Grampa, Marguerite's father, a cobbler of German descent. He came over for Sunday supper bringing marshmallows, and to listen to Paul Rader sermons on the Atwater Kent Radio.

Grams, Marguerite's mother. Rumored her house was marked by vagrants at the Old City Jail as a place where they were never refused a meal, no matter how many showed up.

Aunt Barb, Gram's older sister. Wore fur coat even in the heat of summer, and made grandkids swear to cut off her big toe when she died to make sure she was really dead.

—*continued*

Ray and Marguerite raised seven children:

Ray Junior, very patriotic, he served in two wars, and took over his father's contracting business. Married Lois, children Susan, John, and Robert.

Ruth, born at stroke of midnight October 31. She had a contagious enthusiasm. Throughout her life she was closely involved with all of her family. Her oral history inspired most of these poems. Married Lowell, son James.

Carolyn, for whom family was paramount. Sometimes she attempted to mold others to fit her family vision. Married Perry, daughter Sally.

Alice Patricia, had a zest for life, whatever the consequences. Married Dean, children Jim, Gary, and Jan.

Donna Jean, "Sweet as her Cherry Coke Jell-O," married Wendell and lived together for seventy years in a farmhouse built by her father, Ray, children Wendy and Dirk.

Mary Margaret, the "pride of the family." Teacher, "Her classes-a great adventure." Married George, their land farmed by the same family for over 150 years and counting, children Margaret, Bob, and Jeanie.

James, world traveler, married Marina, a Swiss Beauty, children Jim, Michelle, and Scott.

Other characters: Astra phobic Mrs. Hickey; Mrs. Stewart, the kleptomaniac; Lena Horn, evil vulture eyes; prankster Hank Pree; undertaker and Jazz enthusiast Mr. Houghton; School Principal Cheever; Chet Inskip, tobacco chewing Chief of Police; Miss Rumble, a fire-eating redhead teacher; grocer Jim Pittsford; baker Mr. Plut; J. B. Foot, gardener; beggar Bill; Ike Diekhoff, delivered ice for ice boxes, saving slivers for children on hot summer days; William Hobson, the last survivor of the Civil War; Grade School Janitor and bell ringer Bun Day; hoboes and others.

Jim, the author and grandson of Marguerite and Ray, who opens the family house every Christmas season. Married Jane, children Jamie and Lowell.

About the Author

James Lowell Hall is a practicing physician in Chicago, Illinois. He is married with two children and a quirky German Shepherd, Moli. He is the author of *Good Night Sweetheart Goodnight* and *Lillibridge Houses,* and edits the poetry column "Poetic Ponderings" in *Wilmette Living Magazine.* Every Christmas season he opens the Lillibridge family home in Delavan for a celebration of family.

Printed in the USA
CPSIA information can be obtained
at www.ICGtesting.com
JSHW021022190524
63152JS00004B/20